Please remember that this is a library book,
and that it belongs only temporarily to each
person who uses it. Be considerate. Do
not write in this, or any, library book.

THE ECONOMIC
HISTORY
OF THE UNITED STATES

ECONOMICS FOR TODAY

THE ECONOMIC HISTORY
OF THE UNITED STATES

Thomas O'Toole

Series Editor: M. Barbara Killen
Professor, University of Minnesota

Lerner Publications Company ▪ Minneapolis, Minnesota

ACKOWLEDGMENTS

Jimmy Carter Library, p. 96; Charleston Library Society, Louis Schwartz, p. 30; Cineplex Odeon Corporation, pp. 6-7; Control Data, p. 10 (bottom); EDR Media, p. 10 (top); Eastman Kodak Company, p. 48; Ford Motor Company, p. 61; Frigidaire, WCI Major Appliance Group, p. 78 (top); Henry W. Haverstock, p. 33; Independent Picture Service, pp. 11, 21, 34-35, 44; Lyndon Baines Johnson Library, p. 88; John F. Kennedy Library, p. 84 (top); Harry J. Lerner, p. 89 (bottom); Library of Congress, pp. 10, 12, 22-23, 25, 27, 33, 44, 50, 51, 55 (right), 56, 60, 66; Lockheed pp. 81 (both), 84 (bottom), 90-91; Los Angeles County Pollution Control District, p. 102 (both); Maytag Company, p. 78 (bottom); George Meany Memorial Archives, p. 79; Metropolitan Sports Facilities Commission, p. 85; Minneapolis Public Library Picture Collection, p. 69; National Archives, pp. 47, 62-63, 65, 68, 71, 74-75; National Aeronautics and Space Administration (NASA), p. 83; Nixon Project, National Archives, p. 93; North Carolina Archives, p. 42; Reagan Presidential Materials Staff, p. 96; Karen Sirvaitis, pp. 14-15; South Coast Air Quality Management District, Lawrence Kolozak, p. 89 (top); Standard Oil Company (N.J.), pp. 54, 55 (left), 59; The Toro Company, p. 85; University of Florida, Solar Energy and Energy Conversion Laboratory, p. 103; UPI/Bettmann Newsphotos, p. 95; Virginia Museum of Fine Arts, Gift of Colonel and Mrs. Edgar W. Garbisch, p. 37; Western Union Corporation, p. 40; White Castle, p. 101.

Front cover photo courtesy of the National Archives; back cover photo courtesy of the Department of Defense.

Library of Congress Cataloging-in-Publication Data

O'Toole, Thomas 1941-
   Economic history of the United States / Thomas O'Toole.
     p.   cm.—(Economics for today)
   Includes index.
   Summary: Describes the origins of the economy of the United States, analyzes its present state of economics, and forecasts the future of our economy.
   ISBN 0-8825-1776-0 (lib. bdg.)
   1. United States—Economic conditions—Juvenile literature. [1. United States—Economic conditions.] I. Title.
HC103.086   1990   89-36993
330.973-dc20   CIP
                                       AC

Manufactured in the United States of America

1 2 3 4 5 6 7 8 9 10 99 98 97 96 95 94 93 92 91 90

CONTENTS

1 Introduction 7

2 European Origins 15

3 A Growing Economy
in the North American Colonies
(1607-1775) 23

4 Building a National Economy
(1776-1865) 35

5 Industrialization, Growth, and
Instability (1866-1929) 49

6 The Crash through the New Deal
(1929-1940) 63

7 World War II through the
Great Society (1941-1968) 75

8 Facing a Challenging Situation
(1969-Present) 91

Glossary 104

Index 111

INTRODUCTION

Can you imagine a world without electricity, gasoline, or hot and cold water from the faucet? Can you imagine a world without supermarkets, shopping malls, or video stores? In such a world, we wouldn't watch television or drive cars, and we would probably not bathe or shower every day. In a world like that, where would we get our food, buy our clothes, or find our entertainment?

Four hundred years ago, everyone lived in such a world, and there are still many parts of the world where most people don't have these things. The goal of this book is to help you understand the changes that have taken place in the United States from the time the country became part of a worldwide economic system until it grew into the economic power that it is now.

During its early years, this country was economically **underdeveloped**. But factories, businesses, and banks grew rapidly from the 1800s until 1914, when the United States developed the most powerful **economy** in the world. This process of change and growth still continues.

The energy and brains of U.S. **entrepreneurs** are almost always praised in history books. But sometimes these books overlook some important things. For example, it is easy to forget the advantages many businesses, farms, and factories had when they began. We are often told that the people of the United States created their great wealth by themselves. This view disregards the help the United States received from British and Western European ideas, money, and experience. It also ignores the plentiful natural resources the United States had and the assistance that some individuals received from the government.

Many things help shape a country's economy. In colonial times, North America was fortunate to have many conditions favorable to developing a strong economy. An economic historian studies these conditions.

One thing an economic historian studies about a country is its physical environment. Where is the country located in the world? How big is it? What is its climate? What are its natural resources—minerals, forests, water, and quality of land?

Next the economic historian looks at human resources: the **producers** who make and supply goods and services and the **consumers** who buy or use them. He or she studies the size of the population, the number of people

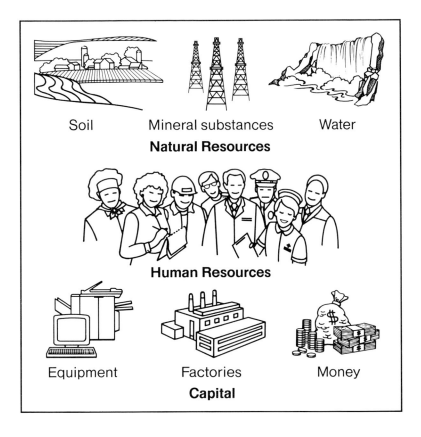

| Soil | Mineral substances | Water |

Natural Resources

Human Resources

| Equipment | Factories | Money |

Capital

who are able to work, the skills and education they have, and how efficient and productive the people are. For example, do they know how to design computers or are they more skilled in creating reed mats?

A third consideration is the economy's **capital**—the equipment (such as trucks) labor uses and the money that buys the equipment. How much capital does the country have? How fast does new capital become available? People's attitudes toward economic growth are also important. Do people want to work hard and become rich? Do they measure success by how many material

*A country's economy depends in part on the skills and education of
the people who live there.*

possessions they can buy? Are they willing to take risks? Can they figure out the best way to increase production?

When discussing the economic history of the United States, it is important to look not only at the achievements of the Europeans but also at the contributions and influence of the Native Americans. Many of the pioneers' trails and village sites, plants used for medicine, foods, crops, and inventions were contributed by Native Americans. Without their help, the European settlers might not have survived on New England's rocky shore.

Most Native Americans had a very different view about the ownership of land from that of the Europeans.

Many colonists might not have survived in the United States without the help of Native Americans.

Colonists purchased land from the Native Americans. The two groups had different views of land ownership.

To many Native Americans, land was almost a living being. They saw the earth as their mother and treated it with respect. Land could not be owned by any individual.

In contrast, by 1600 all the land in Europe was owned by a few wealthy people. There was no unowned land. Unlike North America, where animals roamed freely and anyone could hunt them, in Europe hunting was allowed only by landowners. North American timber was free to anyone willing to cut and transport the trees. The colonists from Europe thought land that was not cleared and used for farming was theirs for the taking. Most Native Americans generally felt that land should be used by all but not owned by anyone. These different views of land ownership led to conflict. The Native

Americans' view of the land was largely disregarded by the European settlers, who were interested in land development.

As we prepare to move into the 21st century, people in the United States are among the most prosperous in the world. With an average family income of over $15,000 a year, most people in the United States have never suffered the kind of poverty that is a day-to-day reality in many countries. Natural and human resources and the absence of control by outsiders helped the United States' economy grow.

It is important for the people of the United States to understand their economic choices. This book looks at historical events in terms of economics and explains how those events created the present economic situation.

EUROPEAN ORIGINS

Hot dogs, breakfast cereal, and peanut butter are some products that people produce. These products are then moved to stores, where you can buy them. Have you ever wondered how the people who make these and other products know what you will buy even though they don't know you? When your television doesn't work, why can you or your parents just thumb through *The Yellow Pages* and find two or three television repair shops in your neighborhood? Does a government "Department of Goods and Services" decide what products should go to your supermarket or how many repair shops each neighborhood should have? What links together those who buy products (consumers) and the stores that sell them? What binds the consumers to the companies (producers) that make the things you want to buy?

The answer in the United States is the **market**. Since ancient times, people all over the world have bought and sold goods. The kind of global market system that the United States participates in today, though, is largely the result of developments that took place in Europe (including the British Isles).

The Growth of Kingdoms

A thousand years ago, much of Europe was divided into manors or estates. A small class of people, known as the nobility, controlled these manors. Manors were mainly self-contained economies, complete in themselves. Most people on the manor worked as laborers for the production of food. Many larger manors also had their own

Medieval manors were independent economic units. Each manor produced its own goods.

blacksmiths, weavers, and bakers. Since each manor produced most of its own goods, there was very little **trade**. The nobles who owned land had wealth and power. The larger class of peasants, who lived and worked on the manor but did not own it, had almost no wealth or power. This economic system was simple and changed very little until about 1500.

At that time, a new pattern began to develop in Europe. For centuries, many small nobles had held onto their manors by forming alliances with other nobles and by fighting those who threatened them. Eventually, kings and queens with better-armed and more efficient armies began to gain control over whole groups of manors. Soon, these powerful kings and queens established kingdoms.

Raising and supplying large, well-equipped armies required a **surplus** of goods. In order to get a surplus, most workers had to be put to work making things that could be sold outside the individual manors. Fewer people were left to grow agricultural products. Those who were left were forced to work harder to produce surplus crops. New farming methods also helped increase production. **Profits** from the sale of surplus goods were used to pay for the cost of each kingdom's wars.

For this new system to work, more wealth had to flow into a kingdom than out of it. The kingdoms that gained more than they lost called this a favorable **balance of trade**. They were able to buy imported goods at a low cost and sell the goods they produced at a higher cost. This system was called **mercantilism**. By about 1700, these national economic systems had replaced the old manor system in much of northwestern Europe, especially in the British Isles.

Market Development

The growth of larger markets created an increased need for money. Money had not been important on the manor, where most trade had been done by **barter**, the simple exchange of one product or service for another. However, as the exchange of goods and services for profit grew, so did the need for money.

For example, if you had a kingdom, and your kingdom produced more cloth than the people living there could use, you might be able to trade the cloth for the horses you needed. But what if the neighboring kingdom had no need for cloth? What if all they wanted to trade for your cloth was ship timbers for their navy? You would have to find someone who wanted to trade timber for your cloth. Then you could trade the timber for the horses you wanted. But what if the people with the timber didn't want cloth either? What if they wanted tapestries? Or iron ore?

Money had clearly become a necessity. With money, you could sell your cloth to anyone who wanted it. With the money you received for the cloth, you could buy horses from anyone who had them for sale. And the horse sellers, in turn, could use their money to buy anything they wanted.

Gold and silver were the most common forms of money in those days. They didn't rot or rust, and they were desired by almost all Europeans. In search of more gold and silver, the kings of Europe financed many voyages of discovery during the 15th and 16th centuries.

The desire for cheap supplies of precious metals (as well as other **raw materials**) made long-distance trade increasingly important. But this trade was expensive,

In Patzún, Guatemala, villagers barter (exchange one product for another) at the open-air market.

and to avoid risking their own money, most kings licensed groups of individuals to do their trading.

The companies these individuals created were usually granted a **monopoly**. This meant they were the only companies allowed to trade in a particular part of the world. The Dutch East India Company, for example, was given the right to conduct Holland's trade with India and Indonesia. Joint stock companies were founded to finance these trading activities. A **joint stock company** had many investors who shared the cost of the overseas adventures by buying **stock**. They also shared the profits or losses according to the amount of stock they owned. These companies made it possible to raise the large sums of money continually needed.

The Protestant Reformation (a split from the Roman Catholic Church that took place in the 16th century) was also part of the changing economic pattern in Europe.

Adam Smith challenged mercantilist policies. His ideas formed the basis for capitalist economic systems.

Most Roman Catholic church leaders were used to an economy in which little money was exchanged. They felt that the profit gained in joint ventures was unearned, and therefore this new way of gaining wealth was wrong.

Many people who lived in the cities of northern Europe disagreed with these church leaders. They thought that profits gained in these new companies were reasonable payment for the risks involved in trade. **Stockholders** emphasized economic success as a positive virtue, and accepted **capital investment** as an honorable activity. In time, many wealthy, urban people in northern Europe left the Catholic Church and became Protestants. The seeds of a new economic system that would expand mercantilism had been planted.

Under mercantilism, a company was expected to act in the best interests of the nation that had granted its charter. But sometimes the private interests of the investors conflicted with the interests of the king or queen and nation.

In 1776, Adam Smith, who is usually considered the founder of modern economics, set forth his views on a system to replace mercantilism. This important book was called *An Inquiry into the Nature and Causes of the Wealth of Nations.* In it, he challenged mercantilism, and his ideas formed the basis for capitalist economic thinking until the late 1930s. **Capitalism** is an economic system in which most industries are privately owned and operated for a profit. Smith argued for a **laissez-faire** system—one with no government interference. He said that a capitalist system took care of itself by balancing **supply** and **demand**. People would seek employment in order to buy goods. As more people competed for jobs, wages would fall. And as the cost of labor fell, more people could be hired. Smith thought this would eventually result in full employment. To some extent, it was this process of supply and demand that drove people in Europe to seek employment and profit in what is now the United States.

3

A GROWING ECONOMY IN THE NORTH AMERICAN COLONIES

(1607-1775)

In North America, early English, Dutch, French, and Swedish settlements were established along the northern and central Atlantic coast of the present-day United States. Trading towns soon grew along the coast. The rich fishing grounds off the eastern coast of New England and Canada were also important. Good seaports and broad rivers such as the Hudson, the Connecticut, the Susquehanna, the Delaware, and the James were ideal for nations whose wealth depended on the seagoing trade. These waterways provided transportation to the interior of the country.

Although the climate varies from north to south, it was mild enough to invite European settlement along most of the Atlantic

23

coast. The area north of Virginia had a climate much like that of northwestern Europe. The temperature averaged between 40 and 70 degrees Fahrenheit (4-21 degrees Celsius) annually. Rainfall was 30 to 50 inches (75-125 centimeters) a year, ideal for nonirrigated agriculture. The warm climate extending from Maryland south made that area particularly valuable. People there could grow crops like tobacco, which would not grow in Europe or New England.

The settlers found a wide range of soils and minerals. The many forests provided wood for fuel and housing, both crucial to colonial life. Minerals necessary to the production of gunpowder, iron, glass, paper, and brick were also present. However, the much-sought-after minerals, gold and silver, were present in very limited quantities. This was disappointing to Europeans who had hoped for more.

Animal life was plentiful, however. Deer, ducks, geese, and fish were important food for the people in the colonies. Native Americans, who cultivated a number of important plants, shared their knowledge with the settlers. Native crops of corn, pumpkins, squash, beans, peanuts, watermelons, and a variety of wild plants and fruits soon became common food for the settlers.

By the late 17th century, Sweden and the Netherlands had become preoccupied with colonies and conflicts in other parts of the world. In America, those countries were no longer serious rivals to England. However, the rivalry between the French and the British in North America was not resolved until the middle of the 18th century.

A high birth rate increased the population in the colonies.

Human Resources

In the colonies, Britain's mercantilist policies were aimed at producing a surplus for the mother country. To produce a surplus, a large labor force was needed, but the English colonies had a labor shortage from the time they were established in the early 1600s. The shortage lasted for more than 150 years. Only later, as the population increased through immigration and a high **birth rate**, did production increase.

In contrast, by the 16th century, England had more than enough people to work in the British Isles. In fact, there were not enough jobs in England to absorb all of the people willing to work. This was also true of industries in many other European countries. People had to move to North America and elsewhere to find jobs.

Good seaports and broad rivers were important to trade and transportation to the interior of the country. Climate and soil conditions varied from north to south.

During the early years of settlement, the European population of North America grew rapidly—from about two hundred people (the original settlers of Virginia) to almost two and a quarter million people within 170 years.

The greatest increase in population after 1650 was due to the high birth rate. Colonists married earlier than people in Europe, had more children, and (because of a better diet) enjoyed longer lives than their relatives in Europe. Even with this tremendous population growth, labor remained in short supply.

The colonists used **indentured servants** to help increase the number of laborers. Some indentured servants signed agreements to work for a certain number of years in exchange for ship passage to the colonies and meager food, clothing, and shelter during their service. Other indentured servants were forcibly sent to the colonies

This ad appeared in a Charleston, South Carolina newspaper.

by the English courts because they were debtors or criminals. To attract more settlers, several colonies granted land to indentured servants at the end of their contracts.

The middle and southern colonies did not grant land to their laborers, however. The land near the coast was thought to be too valuable to give away to servants. In the South, many landowners used slave labor to grow profitable crops on plantations. The first black laborers in the English colonies of North America arrived in the 1600s. In spite of the continuing labor shortage, the high cost of slaves limited the number white plantation owners could afford. In the 17th century, however, profits from tobacco, rice, and indigo allowed plantation owners to buy more slaves.

Throughout the colonial period, skilled labor was in high demand, and most historians agree that colonial industry and manufacturing suffered from a serious undersupply. Skilled workers and artisans in North America were able to earn two or three times what they could earn in Europe. Some communities in the British colonies paid craftspersons and professionals a bonus to attract them, just as some rural communities in the United States offer incentives to attract doctors.

Capital Resources

Capital was also scarce. Since practically no precious metals had been discovered in the colonies, a shortage of coined money lasted until the early 19th century. Sometimes people bartered by exchanging one type of good for another. Commodity money was also used. This involved the use of a product, such as fur, salt, or rice, as money. The creation of various forms of paper money also helped. In some areas trade beads (Native American money) were used for a time. The main sources of capital were credit supplied by merchants and paper money printed in the colonies. Productive capital (livestock, farm tools, and farm equipment) and industrial **capital equipment** were entirely imported at first. These capital goods tended to be owned by wealthy people who remained in Great Britain and charged high prices to the colonists.

Economic Activity of the Colonies

The production of agricultural and other **export** goods, such as lumber, was the chief economic activity in the colonies. Until 1890—over a century after the colonies won independence from England—more people in the United States made a living by farming than by any other occupation. Land was plentiful. Because of Native American crops and techniques, fertile soil, and an agreeable climate, farmers were able to provide for their own needs soon after the first settlements were established. After their needs were met, any surplus could be sold to other colonists and overseas.

New England produced corn, wheat, barley, livestock, and many vegetables and fruits. The middle colonies—New Jersey, Pennsylvania, Maryland, and Delaware—were known as the "Bread Colonies" because of their grain **output**. But they also raised flax, tobacco, farm animals, and a wide variety of fruits, berries, and vegetables. Southern farmers and planters raised food for their own use, but they concentrated on a few major crops, such as tobacco, corn, rice, and indigo.

Although most colonial agricultural goods were used by the people who raised them, there were usually some left to sell. This surplus was exchanged for nonagricultural goods and luxuries such as tea, china, fine cloth, glassware, and other **imports**.

This exchange—of agricultural products produced in the colonies in return for manufactured goods produced in England—was a good example of the mercantilist concept. The people in the northern colonies had an unfavorable balance of trade. This meant that they imported more from England than they sold or exported

Slaves were used to harvest indigo in South Carolina.

to that country. The middle and southern colonies exported more to England, and they might have kept the overall trade in balance. However, the large landowners, particularly in the South, tended to buy many imported items. Many southerners also sent their children to school in England, a practice that was very expensive and represented a large part of the colonial debt—the amount of money the colonies owed England.

The northern colonial merchants, especially those in New England, made their profits by trade (buying and selling goods) rather than by growing and selling crops. They produced few agricultural goods that could be sold for profit in England. Therefore, instead of selling directly to England, they traded in the West Indies, Africa, and southern Europe. With the profit from this trade, they could then pay for the capital and capital equipment they bought from England. Traders from the New England colonies shipped fish, grain, lumber, pine tar (used in shipbuilding), and meat to the Caribbean Islands. They brought back molasses, coined money, fruit, rum, and sugar. These, in turn, were often exchanged at an additional profit for manufactured goods in Europe or slaves in Africa.

Fishing, forestry, and minor manufacturing industries were other economic activities in the colonies. By the time of the American Revolution, one-third of the British trading ships were built in the colonies. The food-processing industry and the construction industry also showed steady expansion during the colonial period, as did the manufacture of simple farm tools.

Economic Independence

The colonists brought the institutions and **technology** of northern Europe to North America. They also learned from the Native Americans and from their own experiences. The settlers used the most appropriate technology available to them.

The settlers had to be self-reliant. In the early years, those who could not adapt often did not survive. The lack of skilled craftspersons in every trade forced people to experiment and invent. They became jacks-of-all-trades just to exist.

Under the protection of the British navy, the colonies prospered. By the time the British defeated the French at the end of the French and Indian wars in 1763, the colonists had formed their own elected assemblies, won certain rights from the colonial governors, and begun to control their internal affairs. They were almost completely independent in economic matters.

After the defeat of France, the British controlled much of North America. But the wars had been expensive, and

Britain also had a **national debt** of about £750 million. To reduce the debt and to help pay for the naval protection that England provided to the colonies, the English Parliament imposed **taxes** on trade and shipping. In an effort to end costly warfare with the Native Americans, England also closed off western land to colonial settlement. At the same time, colonists faced falling prices and unemployment when the wars ended. New England merchants were struggling financially, so the tax was not popular. It was also hard on southern planters, who generally owed money to England. The wealthiest southern colonists began to think that independence from the British and the cancellation of their debts to Britain were good ideas.

More than 150 years had passed since the first English settlement had been established, and new generations of colonists grew up thinking of themselves as American rather than English. Their status as colonials made them politically and economically unequal to the English people who lived in England.

Some planters and merchants had a guaranteed market for the products they shipped to England and other English colonies. Some also enjoyed the protection of shipping provided by the British navy. However, others felt that these benefits were probably offset by restrictions on trade and transportation.

Some southern planters were also angered by rules that said they could ship their sugar, tobacco, and indigo only to England, even when other European markets were paying more. In 1762, the British Parliament passed the Navigation Acts. These new rules required that everything the colonies imported had to come from England, and

This cartoon portrays a tax collector who has been tarred and feathered by a group of Bostonians. They are protesting the increased taxes that England imposed on the colonies.

all goods had to be transported in English ships using primarily English crews.

Many colonists thought that these rules and others were unfair. While most people in the colonies were not in favor of a revolt, political and economic concerns finally led to the American Revolution and independence from the British Empire.

BUILDING A
NATIONAL ECONOMY

During the Revolutionary War, agricultural production was reduced as farmers were called to fight. The war also created some shortages of manufactured goods and food. But those shortages were caused more by transportation problems than by decreases in actual production. Naval blockades by the British and the disruption of overland hauling in battle areas occasionally caused some goods to be held up for long periods of time. Some industries actually profited from the war. They supplied arms, uniforms, boots, and military supplies to the Continental Army.

By 1781, the United States was independent, but its form of government was not yet permanently settled. The Articles of Confederation, the first constitution of the United States, served the country from 1781 through 1789. But the Articles only provided for a "firm league of friendship" among the separate states. The weak central government could not pass laws or impose taxes. Each state set up its own tax system and passed its own laws. These weaknesses limited any economic cooperation among the states.

In the meantime, veterans from the war returned home to find a **depression** and staggering debts. Money owed to them for war service had not been paid. Their farms were being confiscated for lack of **mortgage** payments. Farm prices dropped as soldiers, back on their farms after the war, increased the agricultural labor force and therefore produced more.

Competition from imported manufactured goods (especially British goods) also increased. As British manufacturers went back to producing peacetime products, they again looked for markets in their former North American colonies. With better technology, more capital, and cheaper labor, they were able to supply manufactured goods to North America at prices lower than those in the United States.

A lack of money made the war hard to pay for. State governments printed more paper money to pay their debts. With more paper money in circulation, people tended to charge more for the goods, services, and resources (such as iron ore) they were selling. When prices rose, more money was printed, a cycle called **inflation.**

To complicate things further, the individual states could not agree about the value of their different paper moneys.

The depression followed by inflation created problems. From 1782 to 1785, people in western Massachusetts rebelled against the government. All this led to a growing dissatisfaction with the Articles of Confederation.

Gradually the nation's lawyers, merchants, shippers, land speculators, money lenders, and large landowners began to believe that a strong national government was to their advantage. This belief led to the convention at which a new constitution was written.

The Constitution (1789)

The new plan of government provided a legal and political framework for the establishment of a representative political system that supported a **market economy**. The new government allowed for an economic system in which prices were freely determined by buyers and sellers

George Washington, the presiding officer, addressed the Constitutional Convention in 1787.

rather than by government regulation. The federal (national) government was given broad powers. It could require the payment of taxes and establish a single money system for the whole country. It could also set up **tariffs** (taxes on imported goods) for international trade while eliminating tariffs on trade among states. It protected private property and provided for the enforcement of contracts between individuals or businesses.

By the time all of the states had ratified the Constitution, the nation's economy was much stronger. Commerce and trade within the country were expanding. Manufacturing output was greater than it had been before the Revolutionary War, and farm production continued to yield surpluses. Lack of capital goods and skilled labor, however, continued to limit the rate of economic growth. Since the United States no longer had special trading privileges within the British Empire, the nation's producers faced more competition overseas. But the commercial, farming, and manufacturing foundations of the country were strong and firmly established.

The Constitution laid the legal and political foundation for the development of the United States' economy. The Constitution alone did not determine the course the United States' economy took, but, combined with other factors, it did influence the future development of the economy.

Territorial Expansion

Between 1789 and 1865, the greatest influence on the economic history of the United States was the tremendous growth in the size of the country.

The Louisiana Purchase, the annexation of Texas, the Mexican Cession, the Oregon Treaty, and the Gadsden Purchase expanded the United States to its present continental boundaries and provided huge supplies of natural resources.

The population rapidly swelled. Immigrants poured into the country at an average of 200,000 per year after 1845. By the early 1850s, the yearly number reached 400,000. They provided trained, adult labor for agriculture, construction, and other growing industries. The government promoted land development by selling or giving land to individuals, speculators, toll-road developers, railroad builders, and canal companies. These policies and improved transportation drew over 10 million people—a third of the population—west of the Mississippi before the Civil War.

Transportation and Unification

As the frontier of the United States was pushed west to the Pacific Ocean, a single nationwide economy slowly evolved. The economic interests of the western and central states were joined to those of the Atlantic coast. The development of roads, canals, railroads, and the rapid communication of the telegraph helped make this possible.

In the early 1800s, a need for better roads came from people's desire to transport freight and passengers easily and cheaply. After the War of 1812, the federal government sponsored the National Road, a toll road that reached from Cumberland, Maryland, west to Vandalia, Illinois. This route opened up the Ohio River valley for white settlement.

Workers for Western Union put up telegraph lines, which revolutionized communication.

A business **slump** in 1819 and the depression of the 1820s were followed by another **boom-bust** cycle in the 1830s. These events ended congressional support for road building. In New England and the Middle Atlantic states, private builders then joined with state governments to create a fairly complete system of roads. But as money became scarce, road building came to a halt.

Navigable rivers had been a major means of commercial travel since the beginning of European settlement on the Atlantic coast. At the beginning of the 19th century, the steam-powered riverboat cut freight costs and made upstream trips with heavy cargo possible. The river system, coastal shipping, and the Great Lakes linked local markets east of the Mississippi with cheap, dependable transportation.

The government also assisted the communications revolution by helping telegraph companies. Fifty thousand miles of telegraph lines had been erected by 1860. The government also expanded the postal system from 75 post offices in 1790 to over 31,000 in 1866. This helped establish the communication necessary for business and trade to flourish.

Political and Economic Regionalism

Improved transportation and communication helped unify the nation. However, different political and economic patterns still persisted in some parts of the United States. These differences were increased by developments in agriculture and manufacturing during the 19th century.

Agriculture in the North and the South developed quite differently. Many kinds of farm crops had been produced in the South before the Civil War. Most small to medium-sized southern farms produced corn, other grains, livestock, cotton, and food for the local markets. The large plantations, however, contributed the most to the region's income. Their staple crops of tobacco, sugarcane, rice, and cotton supplied two-thirds of the exports from the United States. The sale abroad of these commodities supplied a large share of the capital needed by the United States.

Plantation crops required hand labor, work which couldn't be done by tools or machines. This hand labor was supplied by slaves. Although slave labor was expensive —less than a third of southern farmers owned any slaves— the total slave population had grown close to 4 million by 1860.

Besides the high cost of keeping slaves, plantation owners faced other problems. Plantations required large investments in land. Export crops were subject to unforeseen price drops in world markets. Many plantation owners also spent money for luxuries rather than for production increases. They often found themselves deeply in debt to **financiers** and exporters in the North.

Many southern landowners, like most wealthy people in the United States by the 1840s, expected the federal government to protect their economic interests, including ownership of slaves. The plantation owners also expected the government to maintain low tariffs on the European goods they imported. High tariffs on imported goods would mean that southern growers could buy fewer manufactured goods from overseas in exchange for the crops they sold.

Northern farmers were not nearly as dependent on overseas markets as the large plantation owners of the South. They sold most of their agricultural goods locally and nationally. Farms in the North were relatively small and were operated by the owners and their families. Raising large families to do the work was much cheaper than buying slaves.

The North produced mainly corn, wheat, livestock, and other food products that could be sold. After 1820, improved machinery cut the cost of producing goods. For example, steam-driven power looms enabled workers to make cloth far faster than they had been able to do with hand-operated looms. Better transportation and inexpensive government land policies also cut costs. The growth of urban areas in the Northeast and Middle Atlantic states provided northern farmers with excellent

Plantation crops, such as cotton, required hand labor, which was supplied by slaves.

markets. This led to increased sales of their farm products. Although these farmers produced most of the things they needed, by 1850 they had begun buying more. They exchanged their surplus crops for manufactured goods and farm machinery produced in the Great Lakes and northeastern sections of the country.

Industry in the North had grown a lot by 1860. Most of this industry still involved food processing or other treatment of agricultural products. Flour mills and the manufacture of lumber, boots and shoes, and other leather goods were the biggest industries. Production of iron, steel, tools, and machinery also increased. Between 1840 and 1860, investments in manufacturing jumped 90 percent, and the value of the things produced rose by 85 percent.

In the late 1830s, a wave of bankruptcies led to the Panic of 1837, which resulted in a depression and many business failures. Mill and factory owners began to cut

Through improved machinery, the cost of producing goods was reduced. Above, machines print cotton quicker, cheaper, and better than the old wood-block method.

Unskilled immigrants flocked to the United States and provided a supply of cheap labor.

costs by recruiting their labor from poor, unskilled immigrants, who had been flocking to the United States in ever-increasing numbers. With this apparently endless supply of cheap labor, factory hours remained long, and factory wages were low.

These unskilled laborers wanted to buy products, including imports, at the cheapest possible price. But northern farmers and industrialists wanted high tariffs on goods from abroad to decrease competition for their products. This position also brought the farmers and industrialists into direct conflict with the large landowners in the South, who opposed high tariffs.

In 1860, the election of Abraham Lincoln, a Republican, represented the power of a new political party that opposed the expansion of slavery. Although Lincoln didn't intend to interfere with slavery where it already existed, his election increased the fear of slave owners in the South that their slaves would be freed. By March 1860, seven southern states had seceded (withdrawn) from the Union. Leaders in these states and the four states that followed them formed the Confederate States of America. The seceding states believed that their economic and social system was in danger. President Lincoln believed the South must remain in the Union. When the South Carolina state militia attacked federal troops at Fort Sumter, South Carolina, war began.

The Civil War (1861-65)

With the outbreak of the war, the Union government's demand for ships, ammunition, uniforms, rifles, and cavalry supplies meant expanded production for northern manufacturers. Northern farmers were also encouraged to raise their output. As thousands of men went off to war, shortages of labor forced both industry and agriculture in the North to use more machinery. To pay for the war, the federal government printed more money. With this greater supply of money in circulation, more capital was available to buy machinery. For a short time, this wartime inflation stimulated the northern economy.

Industry in the South, on the other hand, was not able to produce enough goods to supply the Confederacy's war needs. In the closing years of the conflict, southern industry was able to produce enough arms, but by then it was too late. Early in the war, the South could have built up large credits for the purchase of supplies in Europe by quickly shipping its cotton abroad. Instead, the Confederate leaders stopped cotton exports. They thought this would close down British cotton mills. If that happened, they believed British textile manufacturers would demand that the British government help the South win the war so that the manufacturers could once again buy cotton.

Southern leaders were slow to realize that England had stored more than a year's supply of cotton from the 1859 bumper crop. And they never did realize that cotton shipments from India, Algeria, and Russia had been increasing. England simply did not need southern cotton.

Although the South won several early battles, the southern economy did not have the industrial power or organization to last throughout the war. By the time of its surrender in 1865, the region had suffered vast destruction. Cities and towns were in shambles. Fields were unplanted. Horses, cattle, and hogs had been slaughtered. And, as in the North, families had been disrupted and many

Many cities in the South were destroyed during the Civil War.
Above, *Charleston, South Carolina*

young men had been killed. The South experienced an economic collapse and was forced to reorganize, but it had insufficient skilled labor and almost no capital with which to do so.

Though the North also lost many young men, their numbers were rapidly replaced by a flood of immigrants. The South, with its surplus unskilled labor force of freed slaves, attracted far fewer job-seeking immigrants than the North. Agriculture and industry in the North had received major governmental support during the war. Output reached new heights in 1865, and northern industrial production continued to rise, with some interruptions, for the rest of the century.

INDUSTRIALIZATION, GROWTH, AND INSTABILITY

(1866-1929)

After the Civil War, industry expanded faster than ever before. The basic ingredients needed for a large-scale industrial economy—natural resources, adequate labor supply, and sufficient capital—were already present before the war. After the war, they were in greater supply.

The United States had some of the world's richest supplies of timber, coal, iron, and petroleum. Railroads made it possible for people to settle the Great Plains and the Far West. The opening of new farmland and the invention of new farming equipment increased the nation's already large agricultural production and did so with less labor. After the Civil War, unemployed young

Workers, including children, leave after a long day at the factory.

people from the farms and poor southern and eastern European immigrants furnished cheap factory labor.

Northern businesses made large profits during the war. These and the fortunes made in the gold and silver mines made plenty of money (capital) available to invest in industry. Fortunes made in the fur trade, whaling, and other declining industries also contributed to the availability of capital.

Two additional ingredients necessary for a rapidly expanding economy, entrepreneurs and an adequate market, also became apparent after the Civil War. Entrepreneurship is the ability to change an industry or start a new one by putting new ideas and/or technology into productive use. Entrepreneurship and an adequate market helped the **gross national product** (GNP) increase dramatically during the period between the end of the Civil War in 1865 and the crash of 1929. (The GNP is a measure of an economy's output. It includes the total value of all goods and services produced within one year.)

Increasingly after 1865, clever, and sometimes ruthless, entrepreneurs managed natural resources, labor, and capital in the nation's growing businesses. Many of them were former military officers who had had experience with troop movement, payroll operations, and supply problems. Others were civilians. For example, John Pierpont Morgan, who became a famous financier, sold government war bonds to get his start. Andrew Carnegie, a leading steel manufacturer, developed his managerial skills by organizing the Pennsylvania Railroad to move war goods.

John Pierpont Morgan, banker and financier

The final necessity, markets, was furnished by the growing population and a railroad network rapidly spreading across the continent. Personal income and standards of living rose, but not for everyone. In the cities, many working people saw little of the general prosperity of this period. By 1890, the average annual wage of city workers (about $430) had actually declined somewhat. Many farmers on the western frontier were hurt by high **interest** rates. The rural South was also a region of widespread poverty. Many Native Americans lost most of their land during this same period as mining interests and cattle owners moved in.

Industrialization

Before 1860, the production and exchange of goods and services in the U.S. was organized in many small economic units. Most manufacturing and selling was done in companies with fewer than six employees. Between 1880 and 1920, this situation changed.

To make large businesses work well, new forms of organization were needed. Before 1860, individuals or **partnerships** could generally raise enough capital to finance even the largest enterprises of the day. But after 1865, increased production and use of machinery required much larger sums of money. The **corporation** soon replaced the partnership as the most typical kind of industrial organization. A corporation is a business in which many people (stockholders) invest money. Each person owns stock in the business and receives part of the profits (**dividends**) according to how many **shares** of stock she or he owns.

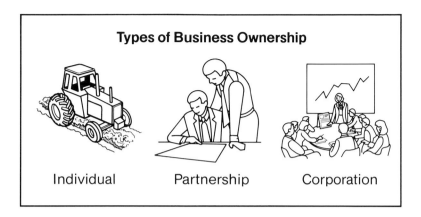

Types of Business Ownership

Individual   Partnership   Corporation

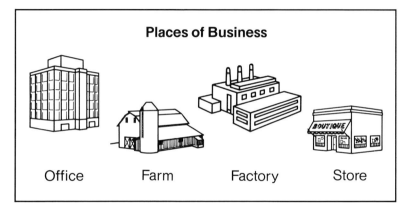

Places of Business

Office   Farm   Factory   Store

The value of manufactured products in the United States, $2.4 billion in 1896, rose to $24 billion by the end of 1914. In 1929 the figure reached over $70 billion. The amount, or volume, of manufactured goods increased 300 percent during that same period. The labor force, however, rose by only 16 percent. This big increase in production was a result of a shift in the labor force. Many of the nation's workers, almost 40 percent, changed from farming to manufacturing jobs. The three most important industries were railroads, iron and steel, and petroleum.

Substantial profits in many industries led to the development of the **trust**, or **holding company**. A trust is an organization controlling several companies that produce the same product. For example, in 1882, the Standard Oil Trust, the forerunner of Exxon, was established by John D. Rockefeller, and it dominated the oil industry in the United States. Trusts led to great concentrations of wealth in the hands of a very few people. When one corporation controls a major portion of an industry, it becomes a monopoly because it has no competition. Monopolies led to extremely low prices to eliminate competition, then higher costs for the consumer, and careless use of the nation's resources.

Some of the most striking businesspeople in the age of **industrialization** in the United States were called

Standard Oil dominated the U.S. oil industry. Some Texas wells are shown here.

John D. Rockefeller, left, *and Cornelius Vanderbilt,* right

robber barons because of their ruthless business practices. They wrestled for greater and greater control of the economy. Cornelius Vanderbilt, who made his fortune in shipping and commerce before the Civil War, emerged after the war as one of the first railway kings. Vanderbilt allowed no opposition. When state legislatures opposed him, he bribed them. When consumers opposed him, he ignored them. And when other "robber barons" threatened his interests, he ruined them.

The problems that grew out of these ruthless struggles for power finally became so bad that the government had to step in. The Interstate Commerce Commission (ICC), established in 1887, was the first of more than a dozen regulatory commissions. These commissions were given the authority to regulate prices, standards of performance, and operating practices in industries that directly affect the public interest—railroads, electric power, gas pipelines, radio, television, and aviation. The

This cartoon shows the power of monopolistic trusts.

ICC, though somewhat weakened in recent years, remains an important agency.

With the Sherman Antitrust Act of 1890 and the Clayton Act of 1914, the government tried to keep some competition in the marketplace. These government acts made it illegal for trusts and monopolies to set arbitrary prices (prices with no relationship to cost and supply), interfere with competition, or discriminate against certain buyers while favoring others.

Although enforcement of these laws was slow in getting started, their enactment marked a shift from pure laissez-faire capitalism in the United States. Before the rise of big business, many people believed that the forces of competition alone were strong enough to keep a capitalist system functioning smoothly. Many people in the United States thought that the government should restrict its activities to providing police and military protection, postal service, public records, and a sound currency.

Actually, from the colonial period on, local and national governments had been doing much more. They had subsidized and been directly involved in building roads, canals, and railroads and in promoting shipping. They had purchased, sold, and given away vast tracts of land. The federal government had offered tariff protection to certain products and industries, allowed tax rebates (a return of all or a portion of taxes), granted **patents,** and made loans directly to certain businesses. Such governmental interventions are important because they influence the marketplace and can easily be manipulated to the advantage of one business over another.

Clearly, government participation in the economy had been accepted in many areas in the United States. The regulatory commissions and the antitrust legislation, created after 1887, merely added to the government's responsibilities. The government was now charged with policing the marketplace. The protection of the public interest in areas where the forces of competition were inadequate became a government responsibility.

World War I to the Stock Market Crash (1914-29)

When it began, the war between Germany and Great Britain was economically beneficial to the U.S. With both of its main competitors busy with their war, U.S. businesses were free to sell in their competitors' world markets.

Also, both England and Germany needed U.S. manufactured and agricultural goods. But as the war went on, neither country was able to pay its bills in cash.

Rather than stop selling, the U.S. business community started selling on credit. Since England owed more money than Germany, U.S. creditors wanted England, the bigger customer, to win the war in order to collect England's debts. Many people in the United States were upset by German submarine attacks on shipping in the Atlantic as well. In 1917, the United States joined the war on the side of the Allies, convinced that the Germans were the aggressors, and that this was "a war to end all wars."

During the war a Council of National Defense, consisting of the secretaries of war, the navy, agriculture, commerce, labor, and the interior, plus leading businessmen and labor leaders, coordinated the natural and industrial resources of the nation. The Wartime Industries Board planned the national economy by standardizing U.S. production and prices. The Railroads War Board consolidated all railroads into one vast system. Profits were ignored, and the railroad was run strictly for the national interest.

As had been the case after previous wars in U.S. history, World War I ended (in 1918) without anyone looking ahead or planning. Wartime controls on industries were simply ended. No federal assistance was given for the change from military to civilian production. War contracts were cancelled with no advance notice. This abrupt shift meant companies had to produce much less. It caused them to lay off many employees who had no unemployment insurance, and it generally disrupted the economy. Only the rapid growth of four new industries—automobiles, motion pictures, radio, and illegal alcohol—kept the economy from collapsing.

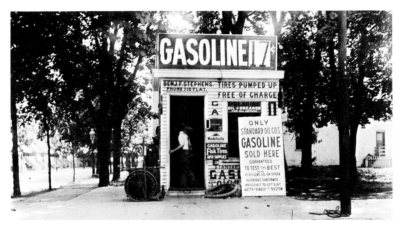

As the auto industry grew, gas stations became important.

The automobile industry employed 5 million people by 1929. Many new subsidiary industries (motels, drive-ins, repair shops, gas stations, an expanded tourist trade, roadside restaurants) also became important.

The motion picture industry, which really started with the formation of United Artists Corporation in 1919, grew tremendously in the following 10 years. One hundred million people were attending the movies each week by 1929. Movie theaters, movie magazines, popcorn production, and soft drink production became important elements in the economy.

Another major new industry was radio. In November 1920, the first station to make regular broadcasts began in Pittsburgh, Pennsylvania. In 1921, $10 million worth of radios were sold. Eight years later, this figure had increased to $400 million. Furthermore, consumer demands for other goods grew as a result of radio advertising.

But the industry that made more money than the other three combined was bootlegging—making and

This still was used by bootleggers to make illegal alcohol in 1922.

supplying illegal alcohol. (In 1920, the 18th Amendment to the Constitution made all alcohol illegal.) Much of the bootlegging industry was controlled by organized crime, and those involved gained tremendous wealth from selling illegal alcohol. Soon the bootleggers moved into other areas of crime as well, especially prostitution and gambling.

The prosperity of the '20s rested on a very weak foundation. Mass-production techniques, such as the **assembly line**, increased the output of goods, but the wages of factory workers did not keep up with the increase in prices. Farmers, minority groups, and many others in the United States benefited little from this increase in production. Farmers were losing **real income** (what a given quantity of money will actually buy) because prices paid for farm products declined. But as long as the purchasing power of large segments of the urban working population didn't decline too much, this discrepancy went unnoticed.

In the long run, the economy was unhealthy. Economists estimate that industrial productivity increased three times as fast as real income from about 1923 to 1929. Many people were lured into buying goods on the installment plan, although they could not afford them. By the late 1920s, urban workers found that credit was no longer available. They joined many farmers and underemployed people in being unable to buy what U.S. industry was producing. Neither Europe nor the rest of the world could afford these goods.

Assembly lines increased production in the auto industry.

6

THE CRASH THROUGH THE NEW DEAL

(1929-1940)

Like other industrial economies, the economy of the United States has experienced periods of growth and prosperity followed by retreat and decline (boom and bust) throughout its history. The depressions of 1837, 1857, 1873, and 1893 were accompanied by financial panics—periods when private citizens and investors lost faith in the economy and quickly withdrew their funds from banks and the stock market. But the depression that followed the **stock market** collapse of 1929 was by far the worst in the history of the United States. Economists and historians tend to agree that the major cause of the crash was an unregulated laissez-faire economy. Unsound business practices had become commonplace, and the nation had come to accept outrageous get-rich-quick schemes.

In the late 1920s, a few people became very rich, but many more became poorer every day. Many laws protected the well-being of the wealthy. Income tax in the higher brackets was reduced, and inheritance and gift taxes (taxes paid on money, property, etc. that a person inherits or is given) were repealed. This helped the rich keep their wealth.

More and more, the national economy came to depend on the consumption of luxury goods and services by the rich. The lower and middle classes were left with less and less buying power. As a result, the economic gap between the upper and lower classes widened as the real income of the average worker declined.

Unfair and monopolistic business practices also contributed to the crash. Businessmen constantly tried to eliminate their competition. Corporate profits soared as large businesses took control of unrelated enterprises to form **conglomerates**, the consolidation of companies in different industries into a single corporation. These conglomerates began to dominate the production of goods— all the way from the raw material stage to the marketplace. Ford Motor Company's attempt to control rubber production in Brazil is a good example. Ford wanted to control all aspects of automobile production, from the rubber needed to make tires to the retail sale of the car.

Many corporations also held stock in competing companies. For example, General Motors invested in Chrysler stock. And banks invested heavily in the future growth and prosperity of many companies. The con-

In New York, panic-stricken crowds filled the streets after the stock market crash of 1929.

tinued well-being of one part of the economy came to depend more and more on the well-being of other parts. In other words, it became interdependent. A major shock to any part of this interlocking system would send much of the structure tumbling down like a pile of toy blocks.

During the First World War, the United States had become a creditor nation (a nation which lent money to other countries). Borrowers in other countries owed considerably more money to the United States than U.S. borrowers owed overseas. In the United States, large lending institutions, such as banks and insurance companies, arranged risky loans to borrowers in many countries.

President Herbert H. Hoover

When leading overseas banks went broke, a wave of bankruptcies and business calamities followed throughout the world as well as in the United States. Investors found that their stocks were worth little or nothing.

The depression that had gripped farmers and other working-class people throughout most of the '20s finally reached the upper and middle classes in the fall of 1929. The economic and political leaders of the United States believed that the laissez-faire market economy would take care of itself. Most business leaders expected the economy to recover automatically, without help from the government. President Herbert Hoover's administration supported tax cuts so consumers would have more money to buy things. Buying more would increase factory orders.

The administration also thought that lower interest rates would increase investment and production. The

Hoover administration wanted to reduce farm surpluses so that there would be a greater demand for farm products. If the demand increased, prices paid to farmers would also increase. To stimulate production, Hoover supported the creation of the Reconstruction Finance Corporation, which made loans to banks, railroads, and insurance companies. The Hoover administration spent $2.5 billion on public works, such as bridge construction, to create jobs. It also gave loans to states for relief programs (food and housing assistance for the very poor), although such aid was considered a violation of U.S. economic tradition.

All of this was too little, too late. It did little good to stimulate production when most people had no money to buy the goods produced. Unemployed workers had nothing to protect them. No government programs existed to give assistance (**unemployment compensation** and **welfare**) to people who were temporarily out of work or who could not support themselves. Many unemployed people had to stand in "soup lines" run by charities to get food and avoid starvation.

By 1932, more than 5,000 banks had failed. They had been unable to repay investors and had gone out of business, wiping out the **savings** of millions of small customers. The banker, once a pillar of society, watched as his home and possessions were sold at auction. Farm prices, already low after a decade of decline, dropped an additional 66 percent. The nation's rural highways were crowded with broken-down trucks and cars piled high with the possessions of farm families, who were fleeing both **foreclosure** and drought and searching for nonexistent work.

Two jobless men read the want ads on a park bench in Washington, D.C., in 1938.

Business failures increased by more than 50 percent, and business profits almost disappeared. People who once owned prosperous businesses sold apples on the streets. Small investors lost $3 billion in 1932 alone. Many people who had dreamed of wealth and security found themselves faced with hungry children and unheated homes. Producers who were unable to sell their goods let their factories stand idle. Workers were laid off. Few jobs were to be found anywhere.

Average weekly wages in manufacturing, which had been slipping throughout the '20s, dropped by as much as 35 percent. Twenty million people were unemployed. Thousands lost their homes because they couldn't afford the mortgage payments. The economic loss was great, and the human suffering was unmatched in U.S. history. In 1932, three times as many people left the United States as immigrated to it. Many of those leaving went to the

Soviet Union. The myth of the United States as the Promised Land was no longer believed by all.

The New Deal

As the Depression continued, the government's failure to provide relief or to get people back to work caused voters to turn to new leadership. When he ran for president in 1932, Franklin Delano Roosevelt promised change. He called his program the **New Deal**.

The New Deal was largely experimental at first, attacking symptoms and seeking causes. Ultimately, it backed away from the total acceptance of laissez-faire economics and adopted some of the policies of John

President Franklin Delano Roosevelt promised change. He called his program the New Deal.

Maynard Keynes, one of the most influential economists of all time. Keynes argued that government spending was necessary to end **recessions** and depressions. In his book *The General Theory of Employment, Interest, and Money,* he said that the government should print or borrow money and pay unemployed people to do various kinds of work. People would then spend the money they earned and get the economy growing again.

In the first three months of 1933, Congress gave President Roosevelt broad powers to adjust the country's money and banking system. Programs to assist farmers and industry were also set up. The Agriculture Adjustment Act attempted to raise the prices of farm products by reducing their supply. The National Industrial Recovery Act regulated the production of other products, the prices of those products, and, more importantly, wages. The government helped business recover by providing low-interest loans and guaranteeing investors a fixed return.

In a clear break with the past, New Deal policy sought first to provide direct relief, then jobs and income for individuals. Leaders of the New Deal realized that when individuals were again earning money, the demand for consumer goods would rise. Economic advisers in the Roosevelt administration thought that government needed to help consumers as well as producers. Once this was done, they thought that the economy would resume its natural activity.

Congress allotted several billion dollars to provide emergency relief. It also set up agencies to create jobs for the unemployed. The Works Progress Administration (WPA), the Public Works Administration (PWA), the

Under the Roosevelt administration, Congress created several agencies to train young people and reduce unemployment.

National Youth Administration (NYA), and the Civilian Conservation Corps (CCC) were part of the "alphabet soup" of agencies created to reduce unemployment during the 1930s.

New Deal programs provided aid for the homeowner and the farmer as well. Credit arrangements to prevent foreclosures on mortgages and insurance plans to protect bank deposits were established. A commission was set up to regulate the stock market. Pension programs for the elderly and unemployment compensation were also created, as well as a new income-tax law, which taxed upper-income groups most heavily.

At the same time, the dollar was **devalued**. The government simply declared that the dollar would be worth a lesser amount of gold than it had previously been. This reduced the exchange value of the dollar. As a result, it took fewer French francs (or other foreign currency) to buy a dollar. This made U.S. goods cheaper on the world market, and the demand for them was expected to go up. If companies had to produce more because of a high demand, they would have to hire more people. This, in turn, would have created more jobs in the United States. In reality, however, the devaluation had little immediate effect, because most of the world's population did not have enough money to feed themselves. They could not afford to buy even the cheaper products of the United States.

The policies of the New Deal were never able to get everyone back to work, but economic conditions were much improved. After eight years of New Deal programs, farm prices were up 22 percent, and agricultural income had almost doubled from the 1933 low. Almost four million unemployed people had gone back to work. No banks had failed since 1934, and foreclosures of home and farm mortgages were fewer than in the 1920s. Wages rose 20 percent overall, and industrial production increased 60 percent between 1933 and 1940.

During that time, the government spent a great deal of money to raise the demand for consumer goods and services. This spending caused the national debt (the total amount of money owed by both the government and private individuals) to increase. It grew from about $16 million in 1929 to $24.9 billion around 1940.

In 1937, however, before the economy was completely

back on its feet, spending was cut back. The **Federal Reserve** (the central bank of the United States) slowed the rate of growth of the money supply. Less money was being put into circulation. That meant there was less money available to businesses that wanted to borrow money for new factories, equipment, and inventory. These businesses could not expand. Unemployment rose again, and consumer demand declined, because people without income cannot afford to buy things.

Under the New Deal, the federal government assumed some responsibility for the welfare of individuals and the economy as a whole. The policies of the New Deal did represent action, and they attacked some of the most unequal aspects of the economy and made it more humane. They broadened the **mixed economy** (one with primarily private ownership, with some areas of government regulation), which had previously focused on promoting big businesses. Although many wealthy people disliked the increased government control, the majority of working people were encouraged by the results. Because of the New Deal, most U.S. citizens continued to believe in their political and economic system, which had evolved over the previous 300 years.

WORLD WAR II THROUGH THE GREAT SOCIETY

(1941-1968)

The entry of the United States into World War II in 1941 greatly increased the demand for all sorts of goods and services. Producers of war materials had experienced almost three years of slow revival before 1941, but production really boomed once the country was officially at war. By 1943, the production of war materials was three times the level of 1939. By buying all the goods and services the economy could produce for the war, the government finally bailed the country out of the Depression. By 1944, the GNP was 70 percent above the 1939 level.

During World War II, the government improved upon the emergency wartime controls pioneered in World War I. It established a wide variety of agencies and boards to coordinate the increased production. This helped factories turn out defense products and move those products around the world to the combat areas where they were needed. Limits were set on wages and prices. Food and other scarce goods (such as gasoline and rubber tires) were rationed. The government issued coupon books which allowed people to buy certain things only in limited amounts. This prevented runaway inflation, because no matter how much money a person was willing to pay, only a certain amount could be purchased and prices could not be increased.

The government also set limits on the profits of the giant corporations and guaranteed minimum necessities to people in the United States. Consumer prices rose only 4.2 percent between April 1943 and August 1945. Government spending accounted for almost half of the record $220 billion GNP at the peak of the war, and most of the goods produced were being consumed in the war effort.

Thousands of women got jobs outside the home for the first time, and the era of the two-income family began. Wages doubled from their depressed 1939 level. With the addition of overtime pay, wages actually increased 53 percent. **Labor unions**, which had been helped by some of the laws passed in the 1930s, grew in membership with the increase in employment.

The Postwar Period

After the war, it appeared that the economy might again undergo a recession, a period of moderate decline in business activities. During the first six months after the war, 70,000 government contracts were cancelled, and 2.5 million workers were fired from their jobs. Wartime controls were ended in June 1946. Soon prices on some items rose as much as 25 percent because of the greater demand for consumer goods and services. High personal incomes, personal savings, labor's wage demands, and corporate profits also pushed up prices.

In 1946, members of Congress were much more aware of the dangers created by the transition from a wartime to a peacetime economy than they had been after World War I. The Employment Act of 1946 was a major response to fears that unemployment might again trigger a depression. Minimum wages, social security, and government-supported housing became accepted by virtually all members of Congress. The general ideas of the New Deal became law when the Employment Act was passed. The government was finally committed to supporting a mixed economic system in which the government plays an active role in the economy.

As a result, high levels of employment and inflation became normal in the postwar years. Consumer demands, which had been held back, first by the depression and then by the war, became great. People wanted the new refrigerators and washing machines they had not been able to buy for many years. A few industries that had been stimulated by wartime research boomed after the war. These included electronics, plastics, television, and synthetic fabrics. Also, after the war, with many European and Japanese plants out of production due to war damage, manufacturers in the United States faced little competition abroad for markets or raw materials.

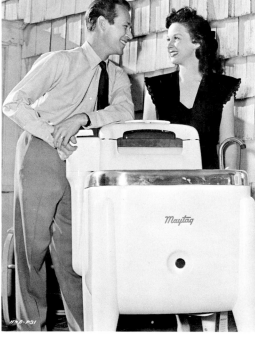

After World War II, consumer demand increased. People wanted things that hadn't been available during the war.

During the 1940s, many unions went on strike for higher wages, as the packinghouse workers, above, did in 1946.

In order to keep pace with the rapid inflation after the war, unions went on **strike** for higher wages. A record 4,985 strikes were called in 1946 alone. Congress passed legislation, such as the Taft-Hartley Act, to regulate powerful unions by permitting companies to hire non-union workers and requiring a cooling-off period before allowing strikes.

Most people's standard of living improved in the postwar years. But the gap increased between middle-class people and those who were not able to find jobs with rising wages. Some people found themselves left further and further behind. Markets were increasing for farm products. To increase profits, large landowners, especially in the South, replaced many farm laborers with machines. People who had lived on the land for generations as sharecroppers (tenant farmers who were provided with housing and food in return for their work) were ordered to leave. These rural families, lacking the skills needed in the new industries, were often forced to take low-paying jobs in towns and cities. The growing prosperity of the middle class hardly touched these latecomers to the industrial society.

The United States began its international aid program on a large scale in the late 1940s with the Marshall Plan. Under this plan, many U.S. corporations invested money and technical assistance in the war-damaged areas of Western Europe. Through the Marshall Plan, business and government restored the German economy and helped the economy of Western Europe. Some historians believe the plan also ensured U.S. companies greater access to the markets and raw materials of former European colonies in Africa, Asia, and Latin America. This economic involvement was also viewed by many in the U.S. as the best way to keep the Soviet Union out of these colonial areas and prevent the spread of Communism.

Since the late 1940s, the political and economic power of the **military-industrial complex** has grown rapidly, creating a system of cooperation between the military (the Defense Department) and large corporations that is beneficial to both. The growing government-business partnerships also increased production and created many new jobs. Business profits soared, and with increased production, inflation was kept to a minimum.

The recessions in 1953, 1957, and 1959 were a very disturbing characteristic of the postwar period. Each recession was accompanied by steadily rising unemployment. Slower growth in the GNP also accompanied these

Part of the military-industrial complex, the Lockheed Corporation built airplanes for use in the Vietnam War.

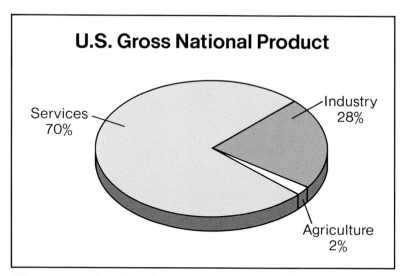

The gross national product (GNP) measures the total amount of goods and services produced by a country during one year. This includes industrial output (things you might buy), services (such as those of teachers and doctors), and agriculture. This graph shows GNP percentages for 1985.

recessions. From 1921 to 1929, the GNP had risen a little less than 4.7 percent a year. From 1947 to 1957, it rose about 3.9 percent a year. Between 1957 and 1962, the output increased less than 3 percent a year. Huge amounts of federal spending kept employment up for the next few years.

The New Frontier

In the presidential campaign of 1960, John F. Kennedy promised "to get the country moving again." His administration's policies, called the **New Frontier,** sought to increase the demand for goods and services, which had declined with the slowing of GNP growth.

One of Kennedy's goals was to land a person on the moon. Astronaut John Young, above, salutes the U.S. flag while standing on the moon's surface.

The federal government increased its spending for housing and urban redevelopment (slum clearance, subsidized housing, and incentives for business to invest in the poor areas of cities). This provided loans and credit to less prosperous regions.

It also expanded the National Aeronautics and Space Administration (NASA). One goal of that program was to land astronauts on the moon before 1970. Another goal was to create more jobs, thereby increasing the amount of money in circulation and stimulating the economy. There were many spin-offs from the space program, such as the growth of the computer industry.

Besides spending money to stimulate the economy, the government tried to stimulate private demand by increasing employment. The government also established **tax incentives** in order to increase industrial output.

President John F. Kennedy

The computer industry was a spin-off of the space program.

Urban development and increased employment were two of the New Frontier goals.

Under these tax laws, private investors were granted tax breaks for investing in the factories and machines necessary to increase production. Tax breaks encouraged businesses to spend money for new factories and equipment, thereby creating more jobs. It also introduced new capital goods into production.

Government spending and the renewed call for troops for the Vietnam War reduced unemployment to about 3.6 percent in 1968. Government spending also triggered higher inflation. The increased demand for consumer goods was created by high employment. But the goods

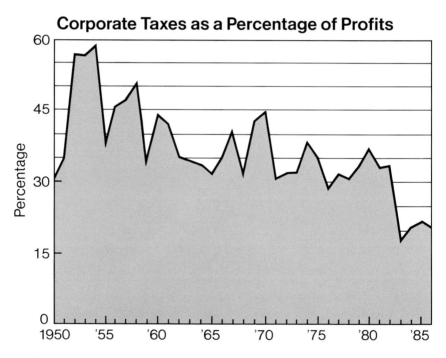

Corporate Taxes as a Percentage of Profits

Source: Center for Popular Economics, *A Field Guide to the U.S Economy.*

Tax incentives encouraged businesses to spend money for factories and equipment in an effort to create more jobs.

people wanted to buy were not always available, because many of the nation's resources were being used to produce war materials rather than consumer goods. In 1968, government leaders took deliberate steps to reduce the amount of money available to consumers, but little could be done to solve the problem completely.

First, the government increased the income tax. With less money to spend, taxpayers could buy fewer consumer goods. This continued the practice of using tax policy as a major tool both to increase and to decrease demand in the United States' economy. The Revenue Act of 1964 had cut personal and corporate taxes in order to leave people more money to spend on consumer goods. With the tax increase of 1968, the government tried to reduce consumer demand and thereby reduce inflation. The tax increase was renewed in 1969 as inflation continued.

Leaders in government also attempted to reduce demand in the late 1960s by reducing the amount of money available for investment. Also, the Federal Reserve raised interest rates, which caused businesses to borrow less money.

The increased taxes and interest rates of the late '60s were less effective in reducing consumer spending than the tax cut of 1964 had been in increasing it. One reason for this was the continued tendency within the U.S. economy to concentrate wealth in the hands of a few people. The richest 10 percent of households in the country received 26.1 percent of the income. The poorest 10 percent received only 1.7 percent. This situation did not help economic growth.

Another reason for the ineffectiveness of the anti-inflation measures in the late 1960s was that the

At a ceremony outside the White House, President Lyndon B. Johnson signed the Economic Opportunity Act of 1964, which created many programs for the poor and unemployed.

government continued its spending. The war in Vietnam, other defense spending, and programs designed to solve some of the problems within the United States' industrial economy all cost money. Cities, which had been the core of industrialization and construction, were beginning to wear out, and they needed rebuilding. A population exceeding 200 million persons required more housing, schools, recreational facilities, and medical care than ever before. Under President Lyndon B. Johnson, the government launched a program which sought to eliminate poverty and build a "**Great Society**." However, growing inflation and increasing national debt led the government to abandon the experiments of the "Great Society" before they were really tried.

By the late 1960s, large cities were beginning to wear out, and many areas needed rebuilding.

FACING
A CHALLENGING
SITUATION

(1969-PRESENT)

Inflation was only one of many problems that Richard Nixon inherited when he took office in 1969 as the 36th president of the United States. President Johnson, who preceded Nixon, had refused to seek a tax increase to finance the rapidly escalating Vietnam War. Borrowing money, rather than taxing, to pay for both the War on Poverty and the Vietnam War led to high inflation by 1966.

Although large amounts of money were being spent by the government, the money wasn't going toward the production of goods and services for the consumer. The money was creating income, however. People wanted to buy things, but they had to

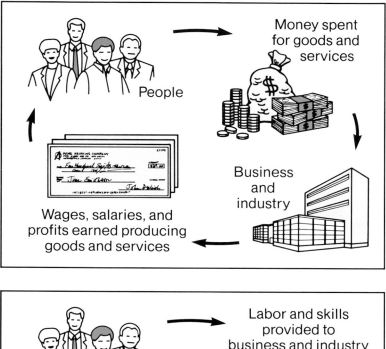

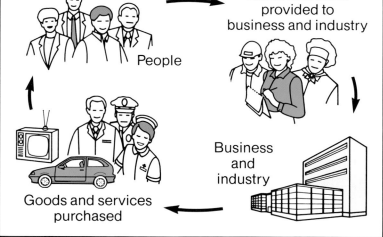

The top chart shows how money flows from people to business and industry and then back to people. The bottom chart shows how people use their skills to produce goods and services at the workplace. The finished goods and services then move from the workplace back to the people.

President Richard M. Nixon

compete for the limited goods available. Buyers' competition for goods drives prices up.

Military spending provides an example of how this cycle works. Many people get jobs in the defense industry. That increases employment. But since defense industries don't produce consumer goods, people have more money available to pay for fewer goods. The resulting inflation threatens the value of the dollar. This, in turn, threatens the nation's role as a great power as well as the quality of life in the United States. People with small incomes suffer because they can't afford to pay the higher prices.

The Nixon administration responded to this economic crisis with a series of cautious attempts to reduce the money supply. By tightening the money supply, the president and his advisers hoped to lower inflation without direct government controls. Instead, inflation continued. Unemployment rose sharply as economic growth slowed.

More unemployment meant that fewer people had money to spend on consumer goods. As people bought less, corporate profits declined. Nervous stockholders withdrew their money from the stock market, and stock prices fell.

Many economists used the term **stagflation** to describe the situation. The first part of this word is derived from *stagnation,* which means inactivity or lack of motion. The rate of economic growth, which had been fairly rapid for 25 years after World War II, had slowed to a crawl. According to economic theory, when this happens, prices should stop rising, or at least should slow their rate of increase. But the opposite happened. The U.S. had a bad case of *inflation,* which provides the second part of the word stagflation.

The 1970s

In the 1970s, people in the United States became more and more aware that laissez-faire/free market policies alone would not solve the nation's economic problems. In 1971, Nixon agreed to borrow money and increase government spending. He established government rules for setting prices and wages. Soon afterward, the policy changed to one of simply asking business to set voluntary limits on prices and wages. Then policy changed back again to one of government rules. The administration's economic policies zigzagged from one policy to the next and back. President Nixon was unable to get the economy of the United States back on course.

In 1974, the country was hit by the worst recession in over 30 years. This recession followed a dramatic increase in the price of oil. The Organization of Petroleum

In 1979, OPEC increased the cost of oil and limited the amount produced. Consumers had to wait in long lines and pay high prices for gasoline.

Exporting Countries (OPEC) had quadrupled oil prices in the fall of 1973. The tremendous increase in oil prices increased transportation costs, reduced the number of automobiles sold, and greatly increased the cost of many products made from petroleum. At the same time, prices were increasing by at least 10 percent.

President Nixon's two immediate successors were not much more successful with the economy, although inflation slowed somewhat while President Gerald Ford was in office. When Jimmy Carter took office, budget deficits were increasing rapidly—the government was spending more money than it was taking in. In an attempt to end the recession, the Federal Reserve tried to increase consumer spending and capital investment by

President Jimmy Carter

*President   Ronald
Reagan*

increasing the money supply. However, the increased money supply only caused higher prices, which meant more inflation. In 1979, there was a second oil crisis. Gasoline prices rose to $1.25 a gallon and shortages caused long lines at gas stations.

The Federal Reserve became alarmed at the inflation rate. In October 1979, it raised interest rates to reduce the amount of money in circulation. By the following January, the country was in another recession. At the same time, the annual rate of inflation had reached 18 percent. Stagflation was on a rampage.

The Reagan Revolution

Ronald Reagan, who overwhelmingly defeated President Carter in 1980, offered answers to the country's most pressing economic problems. For too long, he declared, the federal government's motto had been "tax, tax, tax, spend, spend, spend." Reagan felt that government spending was the cause, not the answer, to the nation's economic problems. He believed that only private enterprise could provide meaningful jobs and help economic growth. If the government cut taxes, said Reagan, people would have more money left to spend. They would be more inclined to work harder to earn more money, and production would increase. With more goods available, prices would go down, decreasing the rate of inflation. If inflation meant that there were too many dollars and too few goods, why not produce more goods?

This brand of economics, called **supply-side economics**, was really the flip side of **Keynesian** economics.

Both had the same objective: to stimulate output, or supply. The Keynesians thought the way to do this was to have the government spend more money, which, in turn, would give businesses the incentive to produce more. The supply-siders thought that a cut in tax rates was the answer because it would stimulate production while reducing inflation.

In January 1981, there was another recession. By the time it ended, that recession was the new postwar record holder. By the end of 1982, the unemployment rate had reached nearly 11 percent, a rate not seen since the end of the Depression. But inflation was finally brought under control. During the next four years, both the inflation and unemployment rates fell, and stagflation seemed a thing of the past.

In late 1987, according to Reagan economists, the U.S. economy was expanding at its most rapid rate since 1983. Industrial production was up more than 5 percent. Factory capacity was at peak operating level, and people felt that they could afford to buy things. **Capital spending** was growing at the fastest rate in three years, and profits in manufacturing were the highest since the 1960s. Since 1982, U.S. industrial production had risen over 26 percent. Reagan supporters argued that by 1989, the U.S. economy was in its seventh year of a peacetime recovery. The average rate of growth in the GNP had been nearly 4 percent a year. Over 15 million jobs had been created, and inflation had been cut from 12.6 percent to less than 4 percent.

However, a little more than a year before Reagan left office, the stock market crashed for the second time in this century. On October 19, 1987, the New York stock market plunged 22.6 percent, a larger drop than the worst single day's fall in 1929. This stock market crash affected the economy of the whole world to an even greater extent than the 1929 crash did, because by 1987, the world economy was so interdependent. The United States had become part of a global economy—factors of production in one country were closely linked to those in other countries. The crash in the United States echoed throughout the world with record losses in Japan, Brazil, Britain, West Germany, and elsewhere.

The economy, like many other things, is influenced as much or more by attitudes and expectations about the future as it is by actual measurements. When people feel the country's economy is bleak, they lose confidence in the stock market. They invest less and contribute to a market decline. When people feel the outlook is good, they have confidence in the system and investments increase.

Understandably, the market crash of 1987 was seen differently by supporters of the Reagan administration's economic policies than by its critics. The supporters viewed it as a nasty, but controlled, correction of the economy. They thought it was caused largely by extreme governmental monetary shifts. The harshest critics of "Reaganomics" saw the Crash of 1987 as a mild preview of worse upheavals if policies were not changed.

Every president since 1960 has campaigned for a **balanced budget**, but Ronald Reagan did so more strongly than anyone else. Every president has argued that paying the interest charges on the national debt made less money available for the country's social and defense needs. Just like a family or a private company, the United

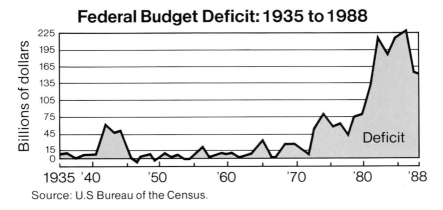

Federal Budget Deficit: 1935 to 1988

Source: U.S Bureau of the Census.

During the Reagan administration, the federal deficit (money owed) increased more than ever before in U.S. history.

States government could not go on financing itself by borrowing money. Nevertheless, the national debt grew more in Reagan's eight-year term than it had in the previous 199 years combined.

By the end of Reagan's administration, the annual *interest* on the national debt was $750 per person. Interest is only the amount paid to borrow money. It does not count toward repayment of the money actually borrowed. At the end of Reagan's term, the U.S. owed more than all the developing nations put together.

At the same time, the United States was importing more than it was exporting. Most economists feel that ideally the country should run a trade balance (an equal balance between what a country imports and what it exports). Until 1975, the United States actually had a trade surplus. It earned more from exporting goods than it spent on buying imports.

In 1968, the United States produced 40 percent of the world's gross product (everything produced in the world).

Although employment increased while Ronald Reagan was president, many of the available jobs were the low-paying, "fast food" type that couldn't support families.

By 1988, it was down to less than 30 percent. In 1968, the United States unmistakably led the world in average per-worker income. By 1988, it was fourth. More people had jobs, but these jobs were often the low-paying, "fast food" type. Critics of Reagan's economic policies argued that his policies hurt the poor and middle class while benefiting the rich and vastly increasing the national debt.

The U.S. economy is one of continual growth, and growth is often accompanied by problems. As people travel faster by car or plane, they face the aggravations of traffic jams and overcrowded airports. The modern conveniences found in many U.S. homes are at the mercy of power shortages and inadequate water supplies. Growth has also brought about dangerous smog, pollution, and other environmental risks. Maybe unchecked economic expansion does not improve the lives of people in the long run.

Is it possible that the world of tomorrow will have less comfortable homes with fewer conveniences? If natural resources are wasted, there is a possibility that tomorrow's world will not even have electricity, gasoline, or many other things currently taken for granted.

Crowding and pollution are only two problems of modern life.

With innovative solutions, many problems of modern life can be solved. Solar energy laboratories, like the one above, hold promise for the future.

In the 21st century, the economy of the United States will be closely connected to the economies of other countries. Large, global companies will probably play an important part in the country's decision-making process, and the U.S. will probably not be able to control its economic destiny as it has in the past. However, given the abundance of human resources and raw materials in the U.S. and a growing international awareness, the economic and social future of the United States and the world is still good, despite many problems.

GLOSSARY

assembly line—a line of factory workers and equipment arranged so that the product being made passes from one operation to the next until it is finished

balance of trade—the relationship between a country's payments for imports and receipts for exports

balanced budget—a budget in which the government's income and expenses are equal

barter—the exchange of goods or services without the use of money

birth rate—the number of births for every hundred persons in a given area during a given time

boom—a period during which business thrives

bust—a period in which business severely declines

capital—money and goods from which income is earned

capital equipment—machinery, tools, and other equipment used in production

capital investment—investment in factories and equipment to increase production

capitalism—an economic system in which most industries are privately owned and operated for a profit. Also called private enterprise, free enterprise, or free market

capital spending—spending for additions or improvements to factories or equipment

conglomerate—the result of the consolidation of companies in different industries into a single corporation

consumer—any person who buys or uses goods and services

corporation—a business that can legally act as a single person, although it may be owned by more than one individual

deficit—a negative balance after expenses are subtracted from income

demand—the amount of a product or service that is wanted at a particular price and time

depression—a relatively long period of very slow business activity, characterized by low prices, low profit levels, low levels of production, and high rates of unemployment

devalue—a process in which the value of currency is reduced in relation to gold, silver, or another country's currency

dividends—profits distributed by a corporation per share of stock owned

economy—the total of all factors that affect the production, sale, and distribution of goods and services

entrepreneurs—people who organize and coordinate land, labor, and capital to produce a profit

export—the sale of goods or services of one country to another

Federal Reserve—the central bank of the U.S. It issues paper money, supervises the banks, and regulates the money supply

financiers—persons who invest large sums of money

foreclosure—a legal measure to end a mortgage because the terms of the mortgage have not been fulfilled

Great Society—the economic and social policies of President Lyndon B. Johnson's administration

gross national product (GNP)—the total value of goods and services produced in a country during a given period of time, usually a year

holding company—a corporation whose objective is to hold enough stock in other corporations to control them

imports—goods purchased from another country

indentured servants—in United States history, these were people who agreed to work for someone for a certain number of years in exchange for passage to North America

industrialization—the shift from nonmechanized to mechanized production of goods

inflation—a widespread rise in prices

interdependent—dependent upon one another

interest—the charge for borrowed money, usually a percentage of the amount borrowed

joint stock company—a business made up of individuals who jointly own the stock of a company

Keynesian—influenced by theories and policies developed by John Maynard Keynes

labor union—an organization of workers whose goals are to improve working conditions and wages

laissez-faire—a French term applied to an economic ideal in which there is no government intervention in economic affairs

market (marketplace)—a network of dealings between buyers and sellers

market economy—an economic system in which prices are determined by the buyers and sellers

mercantilism—an economic theory developed in Europe during the 1600s and 1700s that held that a nation should export more than it imports in order to increase its wealth

military-industrial complex—the system of mutual interests and personnel that has developed between the Department of Defense and the major industries supplying it

mixed economy—a market system in which both the private sector and the government sector take an active role in planning the production of an economy

monopoly—a company that is the only seller of a good or a service and therefore has considerable control over price and output

mortgage—a transfer of property as security for the payment of a debt with an agreement that the transfer is void when the debt is paid

national debt—the debt owed by the national government

New Deal—the social and economic policies of President Franklin D. Roosevelt's administration

New Frontier—the social and economic policies of President John F. Kennedy's administration

output—the amount that is produced

partnership—a business enterprise with two or more owners who share specific rights and responsibilities

patent—a legal document giving an investor the sole rights to an invention

private enterprise—see capitalism

producers—those who make goods or perform services

profits—the money that's left after expenses are deducted

raw materials—unprocessed natural products used in manufacture

real income—income adjusted for changes in the prices of goods and services

recession—a period of decline in the level of business activity

robber barons—a term applied to certain business leaders noted for their ruthless business practices in the late 1800s and early 1900s

savings—personal income that is not spent; also the retained income of businesses

shares—units of ownership in a corporation

slump—a short, sharp period of decline in the level of business activity

speculators—people who purchase goods or capital hoping to sell them at a profit, rather than use them for production or consumption

stagflation—high unemployment and inflation at the same time

stock—a small part of ownership in a corporation. A corporation's stock is usually divided into **shares**.

stockholder—a person who owns stock in a corporation

stock market—the market in which shares of stock in companies are bought and sold

strike—a deliberate work stoppage by workers to force employers to do something such as increase wages

supply—the amount of goods or services that producers offer for sale at any given time

supply-side economics—a view of economics that is more concerned with production than demand and that opposes government intervention

surplus—goods that remain on the market when supply is higher than demand

tariff—a tax, usually on imported goods

tax incentives—tax programs that are designed to increase investment and spending

taxes—required payments by individuals and companies to the government

technology—the way scientific, technical, and engineering knowledge is used to produce goods

trade—the exchange of goods and services among people, regions, or nations

trust—money or property held by an individual or financial institution for another individual, group, or institution

underdeveloped—an economy that produces less than it could, given its factors of production

unemployment compensation—money to assist people who are temporarily out of work

unions—see labor unions

welfare—assistance to people who cannot support themselves

INDEX

agriculture, colonial, 24-25, 27-29, 34-35; northern, 42-43, 46-47; southern, 41-42; 20th century, 60-61, 67, 70, 79

Agricultural Adjustment Act, 70

American Revolution, 31, 33, 35

Articles of Confederation, 36-37

banks, 8, 63-67, 72

canals, 39

capitalism, 21, 56

Carter, Jimmy, 95-97

Civil Conservation Corps, 71

Civil War, 45-47

Clayton Act, 56

Constitution of the United States, 37-38

Depression, 69, 75

Dutch East India Company, 19

Employment Act, 77

entrepreneurs, 8, 50-51

Federal Reserve, 73, 87, 97

Ford, Gerald R., 95

French and Indian wars, 31

Gadsden Purchase, 39

Great Society, 86-89

Hoover, Herbert, 66-67

immigration, 39, 44-45

indentured servants, 26-27

industry, colonial, 28, 31, 35; northern, 43-47, 50; southern, 46-47; 19th century, 49, 52-55; 20th century, 58-61, 70

Interstate Commerce Commission (ICC), 55

Johnson, Lyndon B., 89, 91

Kennedy, John F., 82, 84

Keynes, John Maynard, 70, 98

labor unions, 76, 79

laissez-faire policy, 21, 56, 63, 66, 69, 94

Louisiana Purchase, 39

manors, 17-18

Marshall Plan, 80

mercantilism, 17, 20-21, 25

Mexican Cession, 39

military-industrial complex, 80

money, 18-20, 28, 30, 36, 38, 40, 46, 50, 66-67, 70, 72-73, 84, 86-87, 91, 93-94, 97-98, 100

monopoly, 19

Morgan, John Pierpont, 51

National Industrial Recovery Act, 70
National Youth Administration, 71
Navigation Acts, 32
New Deal, 69-73
New Frontier, 82-85
Nixon, Richard M., 91, 93-95

Oregon Treaty, 39
Organization of Petroleum Exporting Countries (OPEC), 94-95

Protestant Reformation, 20
Public Works Administration, 70

railroads, 34-35, 39, 49, 52, 55, 57-58, 67
Reagan, Ronald W., 96-101
Reconstruction Finance Corporation, 67
Revenue Act of 1984, 87

roads, 39-40, 57
Rockefeller, John D., 54-55
Roosevelt, Franklin Delano, 69-70

Sherman Antitrust Act, 56
slavery, 27-28, 42, 45
Smith, Adam, 20-21
stock market, 57, 63, 71, 94, 99
supply-side economics, 98

Taft-Hartley Act, 79
telegraph, 39, 41
trade, 17-20, 23, 28-32, 38, 41, 101

Vanderbilt, Cornelius, 55
Vietnam War, 86, 88, 90-91

Works Progress Administration, 70
World War I, 57-58, 65, 76-77
World War II, 75, 94

DATE DUE

OCT 2 7 1999			
OC 27 0			
GAYLORD			PRINTED IN U.S.A.